Thanksgiving Energy Vampire

Blasters

DAVID LLOYD STRAUSS

Print ISBN: 979-8-9857860-9-5
eBook ISBN: 979-8-9920658-0-0

First edition
Version 11.2024 | November 2024

SERIES: Energy Vampire Blasters

Published by: Giggle Yoga LLC
PO Box 28
Boulder, CO 80306

All images created with Dalle
Cover Design: Spare Design | Barbara Wade
Ouray, Colorado
Book Production: Book Your Brand LLC

To all the friends and family who bring a little drama to the table—thanks for giving us something to laugh about. Here's to turning the chaos into comedy and making every Thanksgiving a story worth telling!

Contents

How a Falling Rock Turned Me Into an Energy Vampire Blaster

You know those moments when life gives you a sign? Mine came in the form of a falling rock. Not a metaphorical rock, mind you—a literal, out-of-nowhere chunk of the cliff above that decided my head was a great landing spot.

Now, most people would take this as a hint to lie low and maybe invest in a sturdier helmet. But not me. As I recovered (and tried to figure out if the rock had something personal against me), I noticed something interesting. My energy wasn't just being drained by that knock on the noggin—it was disappearing thanks to the real culprits in my life: Energy Vampires.

Energy Vampires are the negative people who thrive on draining your happiness and enthusiasm faster than you can pass the mashed potatoes. They're the Drama Llamas, blowing minor mishaps into full-blown catastrophes. They're the Snide Snipers, firing passive-aggressive comments that leave you second-guessing your gravy. And let's not forget the Inner Vampires—the sneaky voice in your head planting seeds of doubt and insecurity while you're just trying to carve the turkey without losing a finger. These vampires don't drink blood—they feast on your joy, one snarky comment or dramatic sigh at a time.

Recovering from a literal rock to the head taught me that life is full of these sneaky energy drainers. But it also taught me something else: I wasn't about to let them win. If I could survive a rock trying to knock me out of existence, surely, I could take on the Energy Vampire critiquing my cranberry sauce.

And that's how the idea for Energy Vampire Blasters was born.

This book is your secret weapon for dealing with those chaos-causing, joy-stealing, spirit-sucking Energy Vampires who show up at every Thanksgiving table. From passive-aggressive pie critiques to overly dramatic stuffing debates, we're tackling it all. And don't worry, I've thrown in plenty of laughs, because if we can't laugh at the chaos, what's the point?

So, here's to blasting those Energy Vampires with wit, humor, and maybe an extra dollop of whipped cream. Because if a falling rock taught me anything, it's that life is too short to let the turkeys—or the vampires—win.

Let's have some fun, shall we?

Thanksgiving Energy Vampire Blasters

Are you ready to take on the ultimate feast without becoming the main course?

Welcome to the quirky and often chaotic world of *Thanksgiving Energy Vampire Blasters*! Yes, you read that right—this Thanksgiving, it's not just about carving turkeys and passing the cranberry sauce. It's about slicing through the negative vibes and mashing down those energy-sucking creatures who seem to thrive during the holidays.

Thanksgiving—a time for gratitude, family, friends, and, let's face it, a few uninvited emotional freeloaders who feast not on your stuffing, but on your spirit. These Energy Vampires come in all forms: the hovering hostess who can't stop micromanaging, the meddling cousin with unsolicited life advice, the gloomy guest who finds a dark cloud in every silver lining, and let's not forget the ever-present Inner Vampire, lurking in your mind, ready to serve you a big ol' platter of self-doubt.

But here's the good news: You're not defenseless. This isn't a cautionary tale to make you dread the holiday. Nope, this is your secret playbook to tackling Thanksgiving with humor, confidence, and enough energy to still snag that second slice of pie.

Inside these pages, you'll meet the 13 Energy Vampires who are known to crash Thanksgiving festivities—each one more hilariously dreadful than the last. More importantly, you'll learn exactly how to blast them away, reclaim your joy, and keep your holiday table a drama-free zone.

Think of this guide as your trusty toolkit. You'll discover:

- How to spot each Energy Vampire (hint: they're not always as obvious as the one throwing a fit over the cranberry sauce).

- Practical strategies to handle their antics without losing your cool—or your appetite.

- Fun, playful techniques to keep your energy plate full and your emotional well-being intact.

So, grab your metaphorical garlic, sharpen your stakes (or just your wit), and prepare to defend your festive cheer. With this guide, you'll transform from a Thanksgiving survivor into a full-blown Energy Vampire Blaster extraordinaire.

Let's turn those potential energy disasters into delightful moments of merriment. Together, we'll make this Thanksgiving the most joyful, gratitude-filled, and vampire-free feast yet! Ready? Let's dive in and show those Energy Vampires who's boss.

Meet the Original Drama Queens of Thanksgiving

· Your Dinner Table Dishes ·

Before we tackle the Energy Vampires lurking around the table, let's call out the real instigators of Thanksgiving chaos: the dishes themselves. Sure, this holiday is supposed to be about gratitude and togetherness, but let's not pretend the food isn't part of the drama. Each dish has its own personality—flamboyant, comforting, or downright pushy—and together, they create a feast that's practically begging you to go back for seconds, thirds, and "just one more bite." Here's a playful look at the characters on your plate and how overeating might just be the sneakiest Energy Vampire of all.

Mashed Potatoes: The Emotional Manipulator

Soft, comforting, and always there for you, mashed potatoes whisper, "Just one more scoop—don't you deserve this?" Before you know it, you're three servings deep and wondering why your waistband suddenly feels like a bad life choice.

Gravy: The Enabler

Gravy doesn't just smooth over dry turkey; it slides into your thoughts like a persuasive friend. "Go ahead, pour a little more. It's not a meal without me!" It's all fun and games until your plate resembles a gravy swimming pool.

Stuffing: The Overachiever Who Won't Quit

Stuffing isn't satisfied until it's the reason you can't move. "Look at me," it insists, "I've got bread, herbs, sausage, and flavor for days. You can't leave me on the table!" And somehow, you don't.

Cranberry Sauce: The Guilt-Tripper

It sits there, bright and shiny, chirping, "You can't forget me—I'm a classic!" But it's not satisfied with one polite spoonful. Oh no, cranberry sauce demands repeat visits until your plate is an uncomfortable collage of sweet, savory, and regret.

Green Bean Casserole: The Sneaky Overloader

"Hey, I'm veggies!" green bean casserole lies, as if the creamy sauce and crispy onions haven't turned it into a calorie-packed trap. "You're practically eating healthy!" it coaxes, right before you dive in for thirds.

Pumpkin Pie: The Sweet-Talking Closer

Just when you think you can't eat another bite, pumpkin pie winks and says, "Oh, but there's always room for dessert." You believe it, of course, because who can say no to that whipped cream-topped temptation?

Pecan Pie: The Decadent Double-Crosser

Pecan pie doesn't play fair. "I'm rich, I'm bold, and I'm worth every bite," it whispers. And you believe it—right up until you're too full to move.

Dinner Rolls: The Stealthy Saboteur

"Oh, I'm small and harmless," dinner rolls say innocently. But don't let them fool you. By the fourth one slathered in butter, they're the silent co-conspirator in your Thanksgiving food coma.

Sweet Potato Casserole: The Sugary Siren

It doesn't even try to pretend it's healthy. "I'm topped with marshmallows! You need me!" And because it's both dessert and a side dish, it somehow tricks you into thinking it doesn't count.

Turkey: The Heavyweight Champion

The turkey may be the star, but it's also the reason you've reached a level of fullness that feels like a personal challenge. "Keep going," it whispers. "There's more white meat left."

Gravy Boat: The Silent Conspirator

The gravy boat doesn't say much, but it doesn't need to. It just keeps passing by, encouraging you to drench everything on your plate in one last round of indulgence.

Overeating at Thanksgiving doesn't just weigh you down physically—it can steal your energy and joy faster than Aunt Linda can critique your gravy. But the good news? Recognizing this sneaky Energy Vampire is the first step to taking back control.

Now that we've called out the real culprits on your plate, it's time to remember: Thanksgiving isn't a sprint to see how much you can eat—it's a celebration of connection, gratitude, and, yes, delicious food...

in reasonable portions. (Okay, maybe slightly unreasonable, but who's counting?)

Let's savor the flavors without letting them steal the show. And if you find yourself going for a third helping of stuffing, no judgment—just know the Energy Vampires are applauding.

Meet the Uninvited Guests. The 13 Thanksgiving Energy Vampires

Who's coming to dinner? You might be surprised to find out!

As the leaves turn and the air chills, our hearts warm with the anticipation of Thanksgiving—a time to gather, give thanks, and gorge on our favorite seasonal delights. But amidst the bustle of preparation and celebration, lurk guests of a less tangible nature. These aren't your typical plus-ones; they're the Energy Vampires, ready to turn your festive feast into their own personal feeding frenzy.

In this chapter, we're rolling out the not-so-red carpet to introduce you to the 13 types of Energy Vampires you might encounter around your Thanksgiving table. From the sneaky snipers of your serenity to the blatant burglars of bliss, knowing who they are is your first step to keeping your holiday spirits high and your energy securely your own.

1. **The Drama Llama** - Everything is a crisis, whether it's the turkey being slightly overcooked or a minor family squabble. This vampire thrives on the chaos they create and the attention it brings.

2. **The Pessimist Pilgrim** - Nothing is ever quite right for this gloomy guest. Expect lots of sighs and declarations about how things were better last year or how they never turn out.

3. **The Nosy Nester** - Armed with prying questions and a lack of boundaries, this Energy Vampire digs for personal details and stirs up discomfort with their intrusive curiosity.

4. **The Bragging Butterball** - Never missing a beat to tout their own achievements or those of their offspring, this vampire drowns out others' voices with their relentless self-promotion.

5. **The One-Up Turkey** - If you've done it, they've done it better. This vampire can't resist the urge to top every story and steal the spotlight.

6. **The Gloom Monger** - They see the glass half empty, then tip it over. Everything is a catastrophe, and optimism is off their menu.

7. **The Sullen Teen** - Earbuds in, volume up. They suck the energy out of the room by simply disengaging and exuding an aura of indifference.

8. **The Bicker Birds** - This duo brings their personal grievances to the public forum of your dinner table, pecking at each other's faults and past mistakes.

9. **The Judgy Judy** - With a critical eye and hardly a nice word, this vampire scans for faults, freely giving unsolicited advice or passive-aggressive comments.

10. **The Ghosting** - Here one minute, gone the next. This vampire avoids meaningful interactions and leaves others feeling oddly unfulfilled and slightly ignored.

11. **The Martyr Mom** - They've slaved over the stove all day, and they'll make sure everyone knows it. Expect guilt trips served hotter than the gravy.

12. **The Snide Sniper** - Quick with a cutting remark or a cynical joke, this Energy Vampire aims to laugh at others' expenses and often hits a nerve.

13. **The Inner Imp** - Perhaps the most dangerous of all, this is the voice inside your head that whispers you're not enough, that you can't handle the holidays, or that you don't belong.

Each of these Energy Vampires has their own method of sapping the joy from your gathering, but fear not! In the coming chapters, we'll arm you with the tools and tactics to fend off these festive foes, ensuring your Thanksgiving remains a celebration of warmth, gratitude, and genuine connection. Ready your defenses, and let's turn these potential party-poopers into mere footnotes of your holiday cheer!

The Inner Vampire

The Uninvited Grinch of Your Holiday Cheer

Hey, who invited the Inner Vampire to the Thanksgiving feast?

Picture this: you're all set for a spectacular Thanksgiving—turkey roasting to golden perfection, pies cooling on the counter, and the table decked out like something from a magazine. Everything's just perfect—until that niggling voice in your head starts chattering away. Enter the Inner Vampire, your personal fun-sponge, ready to slurp up the holiday spirit faster than you can say "pass the cranberry sauce!"

This isn't your garden-variety party crasher. Nope, the Inner Vampire is a VIP (Very Irritating Pest) with exclusive backstage passes to your brain, stirring up mischief and messing with your mojo. Overcooked the rolls? World-ending catastrophe! Forgot the whipped cream? Might as well call the whole thing off!

How the Inner Vampire Derails Thanksgiving

Thanksgiving is the Inner Vampire's playground. With so many opportunities to stir the pot (literally and figuratively), this sneaky critter can take over your holiday faster than Uncle Bob's snoring takes over the post-dinner couch. Here's how it operates during the big day:

Micromanaging Your Menu: "Are those mashed potatoes too lumpy? Why didn't you add more butter? Everyone's going to notice. Maybe you should just serve bread instead."

Stirring Up Social Anxiety: "What's Cousin Jenna talking about? Oh no, she's looking at you. Quick, think of something clever to say! No, not that. That's awkward."

Feeding on Family Tensions: "Did Aunt Linda just side-eye your centerpiece? Of course she did. She's been judging you since 1995."

Dragging Out Past Mistakes: "Remember that one Thanksgiving when you forgot to defrost the turkey? They're probably still laughing about it."

Cranking Up the Criticism: "Sure, the gravy's great, but don't get too comfortable. Someone will point out how you forgot the sweet potato casserole."

Negative Thoughts Served Up by the Inner Vampire

As soon as the day begins, the Inner Vampire starts cooking up its favorite dish: self-doubt. Here's a sampling of its Thanksgiving specials:

The "Why Bother" Soup: "Everyone's just here for the food anyway. Nobody even notices the effort you put into this."

The Comparison Casserole: "Why can't your table look as fancy as the ones on Instagram? Even your napkins are mismatched."

The Panic Pie: "Did you overcook the turkey? What if it's dry? Oh no, what if it's *too juicy* and gets all over the tablecloth?"

The Existential Cranberry Sauce: "Are these really my family? Why is everyone so crazy? How am I even related to these people?"

The Exit Strategy Gravy: "How long do I have to sit here before it's polite to leave? Can I hide in the bathroom for a while?"

Why the Inner Vampire Loves Thanksgiving

Thanksgiving is the perfect storm of expectations, nostalgia, and high-stakes hosting—all of which the Inner Vampire thrives on. It's not just a holiday; it's a feast for your insecurities:

Pressure to Perform: Between cooking the perfect meal and creating a picture-perfect atmosphere, the Inner Vampire can't resist pointing out every misstep, no matter how minor.

Family Dynamics: The quirks and clashes of family members are ripe for misinterpretation. The Inner Vampire loves to convince you that Aunt Patty's comment about the turkey was *definitely* a jab.

Gratitude Overload: While Thanksgiving is all about being thankful, the Inner Vampire loves to poke holes in the narrative. "Sure, there's a lot to be grateful for—but what about that thing you didn't get right?"

The Inner Vampire's Greatest Hits

If the Inner Vampire had a greatest hits album, these tracks would top the charts every Thanksgiving:

"Are You Even Trying?"
"They All Think You're a Disaster"
"Why Can't You Be Like Them?"
"Everyone's Faking Liking You"
"Is It Over Yet?"

Thanksgiving should be a time of gratitude, joy, and connection, but the Inner Vampire makes it its mission to turn every interaction, every moment of joy, into an opportunity for self-doubt. Recognizing these tactics is the first step in shutting this holiday buzzkill down. For now, let the turkey be the only thing that's roasted this Thanksgiving—not your self-esteem.

The Drama Llama

"Is the turkey slightly dry, or is this the end of the world as we know it?"

Thanksgiving is the perfect stage for the Drama Llama, a master of turning minor mishaps into theatrical meltdowns. The turkey is a tad overcooked? Tragedy of Shakespearean proportions. Uncle Joe didn't RSVP until the last minute? Cue the curtain call of "How could he do this to *me*?" This Energy Vampire doesn't just attend Thanksgiving—they *star* in it, bringing their chaos and flair for dramatics to every corner of the feast.

Who Is the Drama Llama?

The Drama Llama thrives on attention and chaos. They have an uncanny ability to turn the simplest scenarios into headline-worthy crises. They're not necessarily malicious, but their need to be the center of the action means they often stir up unnecessary trouble.

Picture this: The turkey carving starts, and they gasp dramatically. "What's that? A SLIGHTLY pink spot? We're all going to get salmonella!" Everyone stops eating, forks hovering in mid-air, while the Drama Llama launches into a full-blown monologue about holiday mishaps.

Their motto? "Why let a perfectly good moment pass by when I could turn it into a spectacle?"

How the Drama Llama Operates

The Drama Llama has a sixth sense for detecting potential tension—or creating it when things are going too smoothly. Here's how they thrive:

- Minor Mishap, Major Meltdown: They can spot a cracked dinner roll or a slightly wrinkled tablecloth from a mile away and use it to launch a dramatic tirade.

- The Emotional Spotlight: They'll interrupt conversations with exclamations like, "Can you believe this happened to me?" to ensure all eyes are on them.

- Blame Games: They love assigning responsibility for every hiccup. "Well, if *someone* had reminded me about the pie, this wouldn't have happened!"

- Instant Crisis Creation: "Did you hear that? I think the oven just made a weird noise! Oh no, what if it's broken? Thanksgiving is RUINED!"

Drama Llama in Action

Let's set the scene: the family is gathered, the smell of roasted turkey fills the air, and the gravy boat is making its way around the table. The Drama Llama notices a small tear in the napkin they've been handed.

Drama Llama: *"Oh no. Oh no, no, no. How could this happen? A torn napkin on Thanksgiving of all days? It's just so… so disrespectful to the holiday!"*

Cue everyone stopping mid-conversation to reassure them that it's just a napkin. Meanwhile, they milk the moment for all it's worth, complete with dabbing (unnecessary) tears and dramatically folding the napkin into a sad little triangle.

How They Drain Your Energy

Spending time with the Drama Llama feels like you're constantly putting out fires that don't actually exist. Their theatrics divert attention from meaningful moments and leave you emotionally drained. After all, it's exhausting to reassure someone that slightly singed stuffing isn't a sign of the apocalypse.

Tips for Spotting the Drama Llama

You'll recognize the Drama Llama by their go-to phrases:

- "Why does this always happen *to me*?"

- "This is the worst thing that could have happened!"

- "Nobody understands how hard this is!"

They'll also be the ones sighing deeply and looking around to see if anyone's noticing their despair. Spoiler: They want you to notice.

Blasting the Drama Llama

The good news? You don't have to let the Drama Llama's antics ruin your Thanksgiving. Here's how to keep your cool:

- Acknowledge Without Fueling: Offer a quick "Oh, that's unfortunate," but don't dive into their melodrama. Drama Llamas lose steam when their audience doesn't feed into their theatrics.

- Redirect the Spotlight: Shift the conversation to something positive. "The turkey looks amazing, doesn't it? Who wants a second helping?"

- Set Boundaries: If they start spiraling, it's okay to politely steer the conversation back to something neutral. "I think it's time for dessert!"

- Use Humor: Sometimes a little lightheartedness can diffuse the drama. "Oh no, not the napkin tragedy of 2023! We'll write songs about this day."

The Takeaway

The Drama Llama isn't inherently bad—they just have a flair for the dramatic that can derail the holiday vibe. By recognizing their tendencies and handling them with calm, humor, and boundaries, you can keep their theatrics from stealing the show. After all, Thanksgiving is about gratitude, not grandstanding.

So, when the Drama Llama starts their performance, remember: the turkey might be overcooked, but your patience doesn't have to be.

The Pessimist Pilgrim

"Well, last year was better, and next year will probably be worse."

Enter the Pessimist Pilgrim, the Thanksgiving guest who can find a rain cloud in even the sunniest of days. The turkey may be golden, the pies perfectly spiced, and the table beautifully set, but to the Pessimist Pilgrim, it's all just another reminder of how much better things used to be—or how terrible they're sure to become. If negativity were a sport, this Energy Vampire would be an Olympian.

Who Is the Pessimist Pilgrim?

The Pessimist Pilgrim thrives on gloom and doom. They're not necessarily trying to bring everyone else down—it's just their natural state of being. While others are focused on enjoying the moment, the Pessimist Pilgrim is busy cataloging everything that's wrong, might go wrong, or could have been better.

Picture this: The table is filled with laughter, the scent of fresh rolls wafting through the air. Suddenly, the Pessimist Pilgrim sighs dramatically and says, "Remember last year? The turkey was so much juicier than this one. And do you think the gravy is a little too salty?" Cue the awkward silence as the mood dips just a notch.

Their motto? "Why enjoy today when you can reminisce about how much better yesterday was?"

How the Pessimist Pilgrim Operates

The Pessimist Pilgrim has perfected the art of undercutting joy with a few well-timed comments. Here's how they thrive:

- Highlighting Flaws: They'll point out everything from a slightly browned pie crust to the uneven distribution of mashed potatoes on the table.

- Comparing the Past: "It's fine, but it's not like how Grandma used to make it."

- Predicting Disaster: "You know, with how dry this turkey is, someone's going to choke."

- Draining Conversations: They'll steer every discussion into a negative spiral. A chat about the weather? "It's only going to get colder from here." Compliments on the food? "Yeah, but it's a lot of calories, isn't it?"

Pessimist Pilgrim in Action: A Case Study

Let's set the scene: the family is gathered, plates piled high, and the first bites are met with smiles. Just as everyone is about to toast to a wonderful meal, the Pessimist Pilgrim chimes in.

Pessimist Pilgrim: *"Well, it's nice, but I hope you all enjoy it while it lasts. The leftovers never taste as good, and who knows if we'll all even be together next year?"*

Cue the mood shift from festive to slightly morose, as everyone suddenly feels like they're attending a wake instead of a celebration.

How They Drain Your Energy

Spending time with the Pessimist Pilgrim feels like trying to carry a conversation while wearing emotional ankle weights. Their constant negativity creates a sense of heaviness, making it hard to enjoy the lighter, more joyful moments of the day.

Tips for Spotting the Pessimist Pilgrim

You'll recognize the Pessimist Pilgrim by their go-to phrases:

- "It's fine, I guess."

- "Things were so much better before."

- "What's the point? It'll just get worse anyway."

They'll also have a signature sigh that signals their presence, often followed by a complaint disguised as an observation.

Blasting the Pessimist Pilgrim

The good news? You don't have to let the Pessimist Pilgrim bring down your Thanksgiving vibe. Here's how to navigate their negativity:

- Offer a Neutral Acknowledgment: A quick "That's one way to look at it" acknowledges their comment without feeding into their gloom.

- Redirect to Positivity: Shift the focus to something upbeat. "I think this year's pie turned out amazing! What's your favorite part of Thanksgiving dinner?"

- Gently Challenge Their Perspective: Without being confrontational, say something like, "I think there's a lot to appreciate about today. Don't you agree?"

- Keep the Conversation Moving: If their comments start dragging down the mood, steer the discussion elsewhere. "Did anyone catch the game yesterday?"

The Takeaway

The Pessimist Pilgrim isn't trying to ruin Thanksgiving—they just have a knack for seeing the glass as half-empty (and cracked). By keeping their negativity in check and steering the conversation back to gratitude and joy, you can keep their energy-sapping tendencies from taking over the holiday.

So, when the Pessimist Pilgrim starts sighing about the turkey's seasoning or reminiscing about how things used to be, remember: your holiday cheer is too precious to let a little pessimism spoil the feast.

The Nosy Nester

"So, when are you getting married? And why aren't you making more money?"

Thanksgiving is a time for sharing, but for the Nosy Nester, it's open season on your personal life. Armed with prying questions and an unrelenting curiosity, this Energy Vampire loves to dig into topics that have no business being discussed over stuffing and gravy. From your relationship status to your salary, nothing is off-limits when the Nosy Nester is at the table.

Who Is the Nosy Nester?

The Nosy Nester thrives on discomfort—yours, specifically. They're not necessarily trying to be malicious; in their minds, they're just being "interested." But their lack of boundaries and knack for poking into sensitive areas can leave you squirming faster than a turkey in the oven.

Picture this: You're enjoying a bite of cranberry sauce when the Nosy Nester leans in, eyes gleaming with curiosity. "So, are you still single? Why don't you try online dating? My neighbor's son met his wife that way!" Suddenly, you're stuck trying to answer politely while wishing for a trapdoor under your chair.

Their motto? "Sharing is caring—especially when it's *your* business!"

How the Nosy Nester Operates

The Nosy Nester has an arsenal of intrusive tactics that make you feel like you're on trial. Here's how they thrive:

- Asking Loaded Questions: "When are you going to get a real job?" or "Don't you want kids?"

- Offering Unsolicited Advice: They follow up their probing questions with "helpful" tips you never asked for.

- Pivoting Back to You: No matter how much you try to redirect the conversation; they'll find their way back to interrogating you.

- Inviting Gossip: They're not just after your secrets—they want to compare notes with other guests, too.

Nosy Nester in Action: A Case Study

Let's set the scene: The meal is in full swing, and the Nosy Nester is quietly biding their time. Just as you take a sip of wine, they pounce.

Nosy Nester: *"So, how's that job of yours going? Are you still at the same company? I heard layoffs are happening—are you worried?"*

Your mind races as you attempt to deflect, but the Nosy Nester doubles down. "You should really consider going back to school. My friend's daughter did, and now she's making six figures!"

Cue your silent scream as you try to escape their line of fire.

How They Drain Your Energy

Interacting with the Nosy Nester feels like running a conversational obstacle course. Their relentless questioning and lack of tact can leave you feeling flustered, defensive, and emotionally drained. By the time dessert rolls around, you're too exhausted to enjoy it.

Tips for Spotting the Nosy Nester

You'll recognize the Nosy Nester by their go-to phrases:

- "I'm just curious…"

- "Why haven't you…?"

- "Wouldn't you be happier if…?"

They'll also lean in slightly, their eyes gleaming with the thrill of uncovering your secrets.

Blasting the Nosy Nester

The good news? You don't have to spill your deepest secrets just to keep the Nosy Nester satisfied. Here's how to handle their prying questions:

- Give Vague Answers: Keep it light and noncommittal. "Oh, things are going great, thanks for asking!"

- Deflect with Humor: A playful response like, "Wow, you've got more questions than a game of Trivial Pursuit!" can lighten the mood and set boundaries.

- Redirect the Conversation: Turn the spotlight back on them. "Enough about me—how's your garden coming along?"

- Set Firm Boundaries: If they persist, it's okay to politely shut it down. "I'd rather not get into that right now, but thanks for asking."

The Takeaway

The Nosy Nester isn't necessarily trying to cause harm—they're just missing the memo on boundaries. By staying calm, steering the conversation, and keeping your personal life on your terms, you can navigate their questions without letting them ruffle your feathers.

So, when the Nosy Nester starts digging for details about your love life, career, or future plans, remember: your holiday peace is worth protecting, one polite deflection at a time.

The Bragging Butterball

"Did I mention my promotion? And my kids' trophies? And my new car?"

The Bragging Butterball doesn't just arrive at Thanksgiving—they *arrive*. Strutting in with stories of success and achievements, this Energy Vampire turns the dinner table into their personal stage. No matter the topic, they'll find a way to bring it back to themselves, drowning out everyone else's voice with tales of their accomplishments.

Who Is the Bragging Butterball?

The Bragging Butterball thrives on admiration, attention, and the sweet, sweet sound of their own voice. They're not content to let the Thanksgiving vibe flow naturally; they have an agenda, and it's all about showcasing their highlight reel.

Picture this: You're sharing a lighthearted story about a baking mishap, and the Bragging Butterball jumps in. "Oh, speaking of baking, I just whipped up a soufflé for my coworkers, and they said it was restaurant quality. It's not a big deal—people just love my cooking."

Their motto? "Why talk about anything else when you could be talking about *me?*"

How the Bragging Butterball Operates

The Bragging Butterball uses every opportunity to turn the spotlight their way. Here's how they thrive:

- Hijacking Conversations: No matter what you're discussing, they'll interrupt with, "That reminds me of when I..."

- Name-Dropping: "Oh, when I was at that exclusive restaurant last week..." or "You know, my boss personally thanked me for saving the day."

- Comparing Their Best to Your Worst: If you share a challenge, they'll counter with how effortlessly they conquered a similar one.

- Downplaying Others' Contributions: "Your stuffing is great! But have you tried my cranberry sauce? It's won awards in my family."

Bragging Butterball in Action: A Case Study

Let's set the scene: The family is seated, enjoying small talk about the day's events. The Bragging Butterball seizes their moment during the toast.

Bragging Butterball: *"I just want to say how thankful I am for all of you— and for the amazing opportunities I've had this year. My promotion to regional manager has been such a blessing, and did I mention my son's soccer team made it to state championships? Oh, and we just got back from Paris. It's been an incredible year!"*

Cue the collective sigh as everyone tries to steer the conversation back to Thanksgiving.

How They Drain Your Energy

Being around the Bragging Butterball can leave you feeling overshadowed and unheard. Their relentless self-promotion monopolizes the conversation, making it hard for others to share or connect meaningfully. By the time dessert arrives, you might feel more like an audience member than a participant.

Tips for Spotting the Bragging Butterball

You'll recognize the Bragging Butterball by their go-to phrases:

- "Oh, that reminds me of when I…"

- "It's not a big deal, but…"

- "Did I tell you about the time I…"

They'll also have an uncanny ability to steer every topic back to themselves, no matter how unrelated.

Blasting the Bragging Butterball

The good news? You can navigate the Bragging Butterball's self-centered chatter without letting it dominate the holiday. Here's how:

- Redirect the Conversation: Gently steer the topic toward someone else. "That's great! Hey, Uncle Joe, didn't you just finish a big project?"

- Acknowledge Briefly, Then Move On: "Wow, that sounds exciting! So, how's everyone enjoying the stuffing?"

- Limit Their Air Time: If they start monopolizing the table talk, politely interrupt with a group question or activity. "What's everyone's favorite Thanksgiving memory?"

- Keep a Sense of Humor: A playful comment like, "Wow, you've had a busy year—you might need a PR agent!" can lighten the mood while subtly setting boundaries.

The Takeaway

The Bragging Butterball isn't necessarily trying to overshadow everyone—they're just caught up in their own world of achievements. By staying calm, keeping the conversation balanced, and encouraging others to share, you can ensure that their self-promotion doesn't steal the spotlight from the holiday spirit.

So, when the Bragging Butterball starts detailing their latest accomplishments, remember: Thanksgiving is about gratitude and connection—not competing for who's had the most impressive year.

The One-Up Turkey

"You ran a marathon? Well, I ran an ultramarathon. Barefoot."

A h, the One-Up Turkey. The guest who turns every family story into an Olympic event they clearly won. Share a heartfelt memory or a personal achievement? They'll swoop in faster than a Black Friday shopper, determined to prove that whatever you did, they did it bigger, better, and with far more Instagram-worthy results.

Who Is the One-Up Turkey?

The One-Up Turkey is Thanksgiving's unofficial competition committee—all rolled into one overly competitive package. They live for the thrill of topping every tale, stealing the spotlight, and turning conversations into their own personal TED Talk.

Picture this: You casually mention you've started running, and before the mashed potatoes make it down the table, the One-Up Turkey has swooped in. "Oh, you're running? That's great. I actually just finished my third marathon this year. It was rough, but, you know, nothing I couldn't handle."

Their motto? "Anything you can do; I can do better—and I'll make sure everyone knows it."

How the One-Up Turkey Operates

The One-Up Turkey doesn't need an invitation to compete—they'll create one out of thin air. Here's their playbook:

- **Hijacking Stories:** You're mid-sentence sharing a meaningful tale, and they jump in with "Oh, that reminds me of when I…" before you even finish your thought.

- **Dismissing Others' Achievements:** "Oh, you think that's impressive? Wait until you hear about my experience." Their favorite tactic for ensuring the spotlight never leaves their side.

- **Stealing Thunder:** Right as someone's being congratulated, they slide in with, "Well, I also did something pretty amazing last week…"

- **Stretching the Truth:** Their stories always have a hint of embellishment because why stop at the truth when you could win the moment instead?

One-Up Turkey in Action: A Case Study

Let's set the scene: The family is gathered around, sharing highlights from the past year. You proudly mention a recent camping trip that was both challenging and rewarding.

One-Up Turkey: "Camping? Oh, that's cute. Last year, we went backpacking in the Rockies for a week with no guide. It was intense, but we made it through. You really should try something more adventurous next time."

Cue the collective eye-roll as everyone realizes that no story is safe from the One-Up Turkey.

How They Drain Your Energy

Blasting the One-Up Turkey feels like running a conversational obstacle course with no finish line. Their relentless need to outshine everyone can leave you feeling overlooked, overshadowed, and slightly annoyed that you even bothered to share in the first place.

Tips for Spotting the One-Up Turkey

You'll recognize the One-Up Turkey by their classic phrases:

- "Oh, that's nothing compared to…"

- "When I did that, it was way harder."

- "That reminds me of when I…"

They also have a unique ability to swoop into any conversation, turning your wholesome story into the opening act for their grand finale.

Blasting the One-Up Turkey

The good news? You don't have to let the One-Up Turkey dominate the table. Here's how to keep their antics from derailing the holiday:

- **Don't Engage in the Competition:** Resist the urge to compete. A simple "That's cool" acknowledges their story without giving them the validation they crave.

- **Redirect to Someone Else:** Gently shift the focus back to the original storyteller. "That's great, but I really want to hear more about Aunt Sue's trip!"

- **Use Humor to Deflate the Moment:** A playful "Wow, you should write a book!" can add levity while subtly setting a boundary.

- **Set the Tone:** Encourage group sharing with a structured approach. "Let's go around and hear everyone's favorite moment from the year—one at a time!"

The Takeaway

The One-Up Turkey isn't trying to ruin Thanksgiving—they're just trapped in a never-ending competition with everyone, including themselves. By keeping the conversation inclusive and gently steering the spotlight away from their antics, you can ensure that everyone at the table gets their moment to shine.

So, when the One-Up Turkey starts flexing their latest accomplishment, remember: Thanksgiving isn't about winning—it's about celebrating together. Hand them the stuffing, nod politely, and let them bask in their imagined glory. The rest of us will just enjoy the pie.

The Gloom Monger

"The mashed potatoes are cold, and so is my soul."

Meet the Gloom Monger, the Thanksgiving guest who could make a sunny day feel like a funeral. They're the ones sighing over the cranberry sauce, lamenting the state of the world, and reminding everyone how things are "never as good as they used to be." For the Gloom Monger, every silver lining comes with a thunderstorm.

Who Is the Gloom Monger?

The Gloom Monger thrives on pessimism and loves to rain on everyone's Thanksgiving parade. They're not content to quietly endure their gloom—they need to share it, spreading clouds of negativity across the table.

Picture this: The turkey is carved, the plates are full, and everyone's enjoying a lighthearted conversation. Then the Gloom Monger pipes up, "Well, enjoy it while it lasts—everything's going downhill next year." Cue the collective sigh as the mood takes a nosedive.

Their motto? "Why focus on the good when there's so much bad to talk about?"

How the Gloom Monger Operates

The Gloom Monger has a knack for finding the downside in any situation. Here's how they bring the mood down:

- Focusing on Flaws: They'll point out every little imperfection, from a slightly burnt pie crust to a missing chair at the table.

- Predicting Doom: "I heard there's going to be a turkey shortage next year. Enjoy it while you can!"

- Lamenting the Past: "Things were so much better when Grandma hosted Thanksgiving. It just doesn't feel the same anymore."

- Draining Optimism: Any positive comment is met with, "Yeah, but what about...?"

Gloom Monger in Action: A Case Study

Let's set the scene: Everyone's laughing and reminiscing about family traditions when the Gloom Monger strikes.

Gloom Monger: *"It's nice to remember the good times. Too bad things aren't like that anymore. Everything's just so different now."*

The laughter fades as everyone awkwardly nods, unsure how to respond without feeding into the negativity.

How They Drain Your Energy

Spending time with the Gloom Monger feels like trying to swim with an anchor tied to your leg. Their constant negativity makes it hard to stay in a festive mood, leaving you emotionally drained and wondering if you should've stayed home this year.

Tips for Spotting the Gloom Monger

You'll recognize the Gloom Monger by their go-to phrases:

- "It's just not the same anymore."

- "What's the point? Everything's a mess anyway."
- "Enjoy it while it lasts—it probably won't next year."

They'll also be the ones sighing heavily and shaking their head in disapproval at the smallest inconveniences.

Blasting the Gloom Monger

The good news? You can keep the Gloom Monger from casting a shadow over your Thanksgiving. Here's how to handle their negativity:

- Redirect to Positivity: Gently shift the conversation. "That's one way to look at it, but I think we're lucky to be here together. What's everyone's favorite Thanksgiving dish?"

- Don't Get Pulled In: Avoid debating their pessimism—it only fuels their fire. A simple, "That's an interesting perspective," can acknowledge their comment without engaging.

- Use Humor: A playful "Wow, you're really gunning for Most Cheerful Guest award!" can lighten the mood and subtly encourage them to dial it back.

- Focus on the Present: Steer the conversation toward what's happening now. "I think this turkey turned out great—what does everyone think?"

The Takeaway

The Gloom Monger isn't out to ruin Thanksgiving—they just can't help seeing the glass as half empty (or cracked). By redirecting the conversation and keeping the focus on gratitude, you can prevent their gloom from overshadowing the holiday.

So, when the Gloom Monger starts forecasting doom or waxing nostalgic about how much better things used to be, remember: you can't control their outlook, but you can control how much of it you let into your holiday cheer. Thanksgiving is about celebrating the good—even if the Gloom Monger can't quite see it.

The Sullen Teen

"Whatever."

The Sullen Teen doesn't need a microphone or even full sentences to make their presence known—a single dramatic eye roll or heavy sigh is their signature move. This Energy Vampire is a black hole of enthusiasm, pulling everyone else's good vibes into their galaxy of gloom. While others are passing the stuffing and cracking jokes, the Sullen Teen sits there like they've been dragged into an episode of *Thanksgiving Survivor*.

Thanksgiving? More like *Thanks-but-no-thanks*.

Who Is the Sullen Teen?

The Sullen Teen thrives on passive resistance and an air of "don't even think about talking to me." They're not flipping tables or starting arguments—that would take too much effort. Instead, they excel at disengaging. While everyone else is swapping stories or toasting to family, the Sullen Teen is glued to their phone, earbuds in, slouched so far down in their chair they might as well be lying on the floor.

Picture this: While the family dives into a lively conversation about favorite holiday traditions, the Sullen Teen stares at their plate like the mashed potatoes hold the secrets of the universe. Occasionally, they'll glance at their phone, ensuring no one mistakes them for actually enjoying themselves.

Their motto? "I'm here physically, but don't expect much else."

How the Sullen Teen Operates

The Sullen Teen's apathy is their superpower, and they wield it with precision. Here's how they work their mood-draining magic:

- **Minimal Responses:** Their conversational range includes "yeah," "no," and the occasional monotone "whatever."

- **Body Language of Doom:** Slouching, crossed arms, and a death glare that says, "Leave me alone."

- **Screen Obsession:** Their phone is their best friend, their lifeline, and the only thing keeping them tethered to their patience.

- **Silent Judging:** A raised eyebrow or smirk says more than words ever could—and none of it is encouraging.

Sullen Teen in Action

Let's set the scene: The family is going around the table sharing what they're thankful for. When it's the Sullen Teen's turn, they barely lift their head.

Sullen Teen: *"I guess I'm thankful for my phone… and Wi-Fi."*

Cue the collective groan as the rest of the table realizes the Sullen Teen has no plans to engage beyond the absolute minimum effort.

How They Drain Your Energy

Interacting with the Sullen Teen is like talking to a brick wall—except the brick wall is also checking Instagram. Their indifference creates a void at the table, making it harder for others to maintain a lively atmosphere. Instead of basking in holiday cheer, you're left wondering if it's too late to swap them for an extra pumpkin pie.

Tips for Spotting the Sullen Teen

You'll recognize the Sullen Teen by their greatest hits:

- **Monosyllabic Answers:** "Yeah." "No." "Whatever."
- **Eye Rolls and Sighs:** These non-verbal cues are their preferred form of communication.
- **Phone Dependency:** Their phone might as well be surgically attached to their hand—it's their constant companion.

Blasting the Sullen Teen

The good news? You don't have to let the Sullen Teen's apathy drag the whole table down. Here's how to manage their mood with grace:

- **Don't Force Engagement:** Pressuring them to join in will only make them retreat further into their bubble of indifference. Keep the invitation open and low-pressure.
- **Appeal to Their Interests:** Try meeting them where they are. "Hey, what's the funniest thing you've seen on TikTok lately?"
- **Use Humor:** A playful, "Careful, if you smile, you might break something!" can crack through their shell without being confrontational.
- **Let Them Be:** Sometimes the best strategy is to let them stew quietly. Not everyone needs to be the life of the party.

The Takeaway

The Sullen Teen isn't out to ruin Thanksgiving—they're just stuck in their own world of dramatic indifference. By giving them space, keeping the mood light, and letting them engage on their own terms, you can ensure their brooding doesn't overshadow the holiday.

So, when the Sullen Teen sighs loudly or stares blankly into their mashed potatoes, remember: it's not about you. Focus on enjoying the day and let them brood in peace. Who knows? By the time dessert rolls around, you might even get a smile. (No promises.)

The Bicker Birds

"You never listen!" "Well, you never stop talking!"

Thanksgiving just wouldn't feel complete without the Bicker Birds swooping in to add a little drama to the festivities. This dynamic duo has turned squabbling into an art form, turning every minor disagreement into a public spectacle. Forget about carving the turkey or passing the gravy—these two are too busy carving each other's nerves.

Who Are the Bicker Birds?

The Bicker Birds are a pair of professional nitpickers who love to hash out their differences in front of an audience. They don't argue to resolve problems—they argue to keep score and win, no matter how ridiculous the topic.

Picture this: The family is happily passing rolls around the table when the Bicker Birds seize their chance.

Bicker Bird 1: "You *always* forget to refill the water glasses. Why do I have to remind you every year?"

Bicker Bird 2: "Maybe if you stopped micromanaging me, you wouldn't need to!"

Cue the awkward silence as everyone else at the table suddenly becomes *very* interested in their mashed potatoes.

Their motto? "Why let a perfectly good holiday go by when we can argue instead?"

How the Bicker Birds Operate

The Bicker Birds have a special talent for turning private grievances into public drama. Here's how they keep the feathers flying:

- **Revisiting Old Grievances:** "Oh, are you going to mention the time you burned the green bean casserole again? Let it go!"

- **Keeping Score:** They never forget a slight, no matter how small, and they're more than happy to remind each other—and the entire room—about it.

- **Involving the Audience:** They love dragging others into their squabbles with questions like, "Don't you think I'm right about this?"

- **Escalating Quickly:** What starts as a casual comment can spiral into a full-blown squabble faster than you can say "pumpkin pie."

Bicker Birds in Action: A Case Study

Let's set the scene: Dessert is about to be served, and the Bicker Birds spot their opportunity.

Bicker Bird 1: *"You said you'd bake the pie this year, but of course, I ended up doing it—like always."*

Bicker Bird 2: *"Well, maybe if you didn't act like you're the only one who knows how to bake, I'd actually get a chance to help!"*

Cue the collective eye-roll as the rest of the family exchanges uncomfortable glances, silently wondering if they should intervene or just pass the whipped cream.

How They Drain Your Energy

Spending time with the Bicker Birds feels like being caught in the middle of a never-ending ping-pong match where the ball is made of awkward tension. Their constant squabbling creates an uncomfortable atmosphere, leaving everyone else at the table feeling drained and on edge.

Tips for Spotting the Bicker Birds

The Bicker Birds are easy to identify by their signature moves:

- **Rehashing the Past:** They love bringing up old arguments, no matter how irrelevant.

- **Seeking Allies:** They'll try to rope others into the drama with comments like, "Don't you agree with me?"

- **Quick Escalation:** A casual comment can spiral into a heated debate before anyone realizes what's happening.

Blasting the Bicker Birds

The good news? You can manage the Bicker Birds without letting their drama ruffle your feathers. Here's how:

- **Redirect Their Focus:** Shift the conversation to something neutral. "Hey, what's everyone's favorite Thanksgiving tradition?"

- **Use Humor to Diffuse Tension:** A playful "Uh-oh, sounds like we've got a rematch from last Thanksgiving!" can lighten the mood and break the cycle.

- **Avoid Taking Sides:** Stay neutral if they try to drag you into their squabble. A calm, "You both make good points," can keep you out of their crossfire.

- **Change the Subject Entirely:** If all else fails, toss out a random question. "Who wants coffee with their pie?" is a classic lifesaver.

The Takeaway

The Bicker Birds aren't out to ruin Thanksgiving—they're just stuck in a loop of pecking at each other and don't know how to stop. By keeping the focus on positivity and gently steering the conversation away from their squabbles, you can keep the holiday festive and fun.

So, when the Bicker Birds start chirping at each other over who forgot to thaw the turkey or whose fault it is that the stuffing is too salty, remember: their arguments are their problem—not yours. Let them peck it out while you savor your pumpkin pie in peace.

The Judgy Judy

"Oh, that's… an interesting way to carve a turkey."

Judgy Judy isn't here for the food, family bonding, or fun—they're here to critique, one passive-aggressive comment at a time. Whether it's your wine choice, your table settings, or even the way you breathe, this Energy Vampire has their sights set on finding flaws. Armed with a critical eye sharper than your carving knife, Judgy Judy thrives on making you feel just a *little* less confident—all under the guise of "helpful" observations, of course.

Who Is the Judgy Judy?

The Judgy Judy sees the world through a magnifying glass of "meh." They're not outright rude (most of the time), but their subtle digs and faux compliments can leave you second-guessing everything from your mashed potatoes to your life choices. To Judgy Judy, Thanksgiving isn't a holiday—it's a competition, and they've appointed themselves the Simon Cowell of your feast.

Picture this: You proudly bring out your homemade pumpkin pie, and Judgy Judy tilts their head, offers a thin smile, and says, "Oh, did you use canned pumpkin? I suppose that's... convenient." Suddenly, you're wondering if you should've risked the mess of roasting your own pumpkins just to avoid this moment.

Their motto? "I'm not criticizing—I'm just saying!"

How the Judgy Judy Operates

The Judgy Judy thrives on subtlety, delivering their critiques with just enough sugar to make you wonder if you're imagining the sting. Here's how they work their magic:

- **Passive-Aggressive Comments:** "Well, not everyone can make perfect gravy, and that's okay!" (Ouch.)

- **Backhanded Compliments:** "Your outfit is so brave—I could *never* pull that off!" (Was that a compliment or a roast?)

- **Micromanaging Under the Radar:** "Are you sure you want to serve the gravy in that boat? It's a bit... rustic." (Translation: "It looks like you stole it from a flea market.")

- **Comparing to Others:** "You know, Aunt Linda's stuffing always has the perfect seasoning." (Aunt Linda wins, apparently.)

Judgy Judy in Action

Let's set the scene: The table is beautifully set, and everyone's complimenting the effort. Judgy Judy scans the spread, eyes gleaming, and takes their shot.

Judgy Judy: *"Oh, you used paper napkins? That's... practical. I suppose it saves time, doesn't it?"*

Cue the awkward pause as you decide whether to explain your choice or just let the comment hang in the air like an uninvited guest.

How They Drain Your Energy

Spending time with Judgy Judy feels like dodging verbal grenades hidden inside compliments. Every dig chips away at your confidence, making you wonder if your Thanksgiving is less a celebration and more a final exam. Instead of enjoying the moment, you're left overanalyzing everything from your centerpiece to your cranberry sauce.

Tips for Spotting the Judgy Judy

Judgy Judy is easy to spot once you know their tricks. Look out for these signature moves:

- "Oh, that's an *interesting* choice."

- "I'm just trying to help!"

- "Well, if *you're* happy with it, that's what matters."

They'll also deliver their critiques with a sweet smile, as if they're doing you a huge favor by pointing out your flaws.

Blasting the Judgy Judy

The good news? You don't have to let Judgy Judy's remarks stick to you like gravy on your favorite shirt. Here's how to handle them with style:

- **Respond with Confidence:** A cheerful, "Yep, I'm thrilled with how it turned out!" shuts down their critique without leaving room for argument.

- **Use Humor:** Defuse their digs with a playful, "Oh no, the napkin scandal of 2023—I'll never live it down!"

- **Redirect the Focus:** Steer the conversation away from their critique. "Thanks for noticing! So, how's that project you've been working on?"

- **Don't Take the Bait:** Resist the urge to justify your choices. Remember, their comments say more about them than they do about you.

The Takeaway

Judgy Judy isn't trying to be mean—they just can't resist seeing everything as a project in need of improvement. By staying confident, using humor, and redirecting their attention, you can turn their critiques into background noise and keep your holiday vibe intact.

So, when Judgy Judy comments on your paper napkins, the "unique" way you seasoned the stuffing, or your "creative" turkey carving skills, remember: Thanksgiving is about gratitude, not perfection. Let them judge, while you enjoy your pie. (Canned pumpkin and all.)

The Ghosting

"Oh, sorry, I have to take this call!"

The Ghosting is Thanksgiving's greatest mystery. One moment they're nodding along politely, and the next—poof! —they've vanished into thin air. Maybe they're suddenly "needed" in the other room, or perhaps their phone buzzed with a life-or-death Instagram notification. Whatever the excuse, this Energy Vampire's disappearing act leaves everyone scratching their heads and wondering, "Were they even here at all?"

Who Is the Ghosting?

The Ghosting thrives on being just enough present to remind you they exist but never enough to actually connect. They don't do small talk, deep conversations, or family games—they prefer to hover on the edges, occasionally popping in to chuckle or nod before retreating back into the shadows (or their phones). Think of them as the Houdini of holiday gatherings.

Picture this: The family is gathered around, reminiscing about holiday traditions, and someone asks the Ghosting to share a memory. They glance at their phone like it's a bat signal. "Oh, I need to take this—it's work," they mutter before disappearing for the next 20 minutes. The memory? Still unshared.

Their motto? "It's not you—it's me... and my need to be anywhere but here."

How the Ghosting Operates

The Ghosting has an arsenal of stealth tactics that make connecting with them feel like trying to catch a leaf in a windstorm. Here's how they thrive:

- **Phone Shield:** Their phone is their trusty force field, perfect for avoiding eye contact and meaningful conversations.

- **Excuses Galore:** "I need to check on something," "I forgot something in the car," or the classic "I'll be right back!" (Spoiler: They won't.)

- **Silent Presence:** Even when they're at the table, they're distant—nodding vaguely and murmuring agreements without actually contributing.

- **Emotional Evasion:** Personal questions are deflected with vague answers like, "Oh, you know, same old, same old."

The Ghosting in Action

Let's set the scene: The table is buzzing with laughter and conversation, and someone asks the Ghosting for their opinion on the best pie flavor.

Ghosting: *"Oh, I don't know... maybe pecan? Excuse me, I just need to check on something really quick."*

Cue their vanishing act, leaving everyone wondering if they'll be back before dessert—or ever.

How They Drain Your Energy

Interacting with the Ghosting feels like trying to pin down a cloud. Their constant dodging and disappearing create a sense of disconnection, leaving others feeling unimportant and slightly frustrated. Instead of fostering warm, meaningful connections, the Ghosting leaves a chilly void at the table.

Tips for Spotting the Ghosting

The Ghosting has a few telltale habits that make them easy to identify:

- **Always on Their Phone:** Their screen might as well be glued to their hand, and it's always far more interesting than what's happening in the room.

- **Frequent Disappearances:** They're in and out so often you start to wonder if they're playing an elaborate game of hide-and-seek.

- **Minimal Participation:** Their contributions to the conversation are about as substantial as a half-eaten dinner roll—vague nods and murmured agreements at best.

Blasting the Ghosting

The good news? You don't have to let the Ghosting's vanishing act haunt your Thanksgiving. Here's how to handle them without breaking a sweat:

- **Engage on Their Terms:** Instead of diving into deep topics, keep it light. "Seen any good shows lately?" might actually get a response.

- **Make Them Feel Included:** A gentle "We'd love to hear your thoughts" can nudge them into the conversation without overwhelming them.

- **Don't Chase Them Down:** If they disappear, let them. Focus on enjoying the present with the people who are fully engaged.

- **Be Direct if Needed:** If their absence becomes a running joke, a kind but straightforward comment like, "We'd love to have you join us at the table," can work wonders.

The Takeaway

The Ghosting isn't trying to ruin Thanksgiving—they're just uncomfortable with too much togetherness. By letting their distance roll off your back and focusing on the people who *are* engaged, you can keep your holiday spirit intact.

So, when the Ghosting disappears mid-conversation or spends more time scrolling their phone than cutting their pie, remember: their vanishing act doesn't have to steal your joy. Let them haunt the edges of the gathering while you soak up the laughter, love, and second helpings. They'll reappear... probably just in time to grab a to-go box.

The Martyr Mom

"Don't mind me, I'll just clean up everything myself."

Enter the Martyr Mom: part chef, part event planner, and full-time guilt dispenser. This Energy Vampire doesn't just whip up a feast—they whip up a whole performance, complete with dramatic sighs, exaggerated exhaustion, and guilt trips so thick you could serve them with a ladle. Their favorite side dish? Making sure everyone knows exactly how much they've sacrificed to keep the holiday afloat.

Who Is the Martyr Mom?

The Martyr Mom thrives on a potent cocktail of overachievement and self-pity, garnished with a twist of passive-aggression. They genuinely care about making Thanksgiving perfect but want full credit for every ounce of effort—and then some. If you so much as think about relaxing, they'll swoop in with a heavy sigh and a reminder that they've been up since dawn, doing it all for *you*.

Picture this: You're about to dig into your turkey when Martyr Mom appears, balancing three plates like a stressed-out circus act. "I've been on my feet since 5 a.m. making this stuffing. But don't worry—I'm fine. Really."

Their motto? "If I don't suffer for it, is it even Thanksgiving?"

How the Martyr Mom Operates

The Martyr Mom is a master of blending Herculean effort with guilt-laden commentary. Here's how they dominate the holiday stage:

- **The Sigh Symphony:** Every task is accompanied by an audible sigh that could rival a wind tunnel. Setting the table? *Sigh.* Pouring water? *Sigh.*

- **Woe-Is-Me Commentary:** "It's fine—I'll just do it myself. Don't worry about me." Translation: *Absolutely worry about me.*

- **Guilt Garnish:** They sprinkle guilt onto every interaction. "You're just sitting there while I'm running around like a turkey with its head cut off!"

- **The Overworked Hero:** They'll remind everyone that without their hard work, this holiday would've been a total disaster.

Martyr Mom in Action: A Case Study

Let's set the scene: Dinner is winding down, and the compliments are flying. Martyr Mom starts clearing plates like a martyr on a mission.

Martyr Mom: *"Oh, don't get up—I've got it. I mean, I've only been cooking all day and haven't had a chance to sit down once, but it's fine."*

Cue the awkward shuffle as everyone scrambles to offer help, which Martyr Mom accepts with a resigned, "Well, if you insist…"

How They Drain Your Energy

Spending time with the Martyr Mom is like walking through a mine-field of guilt and obligation. Every sigh, every dramatic flourish, and every woe-is-me comment chips away at your ability to just enjoy the holiday. Instead of relaxing, you're left feeling like you should be doing more—even if you've already done plenty.

Tips for Spotting the Martyr Mom

You'll recognize the Martyr Mom by these telltale behaviors:

- **Heavy Sighing:** It's their unofficial theme music.

- **Overdoing It:** They'll make enough food to feed an army, then lament how hard it was to pull off.

- **Subtle Guilt Trips:** "I wish I could sit down and chat, but someone has to keep things running smoothly."

Blasting the Martyr Mom

The good news? You can navigate the Martyr Mom's guilt-laden antics without losing your holiday cheer. Here's how:

- **Offer Help Early:** Beat them to the punch by offering to help before they even start their performance. "Let me take care of the drinks while you finish the appetizers."

- **Compliment Their Efforts:** A genuine "This is incredible—thank you so much for all your hard work" can go a long way in soothing their need for validation.

- **Set Boundaries:** If their martyrdom starts overshadowing the holiday, gently redirect the focus. "You've done so much—now it's time for you to relax and enjoy!"

- **Take Over Without Asking:** Sometimes the best way to help is to jump in and handle a task without waiting for permission.

The Takeaway

Martyr Mom isn't trying to ruin Thanksgiving—they just want to feel appreciated for all their hard work. By offering sincere gratitude, lending a hand where you can, and gently steering the conversation away from their martyrdom, you can keep their antics from draining the holiday spirit.

So, when Martyr Mom starts sighing about how much they've sacrificed or lamenting that no one appreciates them, remember: a little extra patience and a hearty compliment can go a long way toward keeping the peace—and your sanity—intact. Pass the gratitude and save some energy for dessert!

The Snide Sniper

"Well, that's one way to make stuffing, I guess."

The Snide Sniper doesn't show up to Thanksgiving with an empty stomach—they come armed with a quiver of sarcastic remarks and cutting jokes, perfectly aimed to land just where it hurts. Quick with a zinger and even quicker to follow it up with, "Relax, I'm just kidding," this Energy Vampire keeps everyone walking on eggshells while trying not to choke on their mashed potatoes.

Who Is the Snide Sniper?

The Snide Sniper thrives on sly digs and well-placed sarcasm, delivered with the kind of smile that leaves you questioning whether it was a joke or a personal attack. They're not here to throw punches—they're here to throw shade, and they've got Olympic-level aim.

Picture this: You've just set down your beautifully imperfect pumpkin pie, and the Snide Sniper takes their shot. "Oh, going for the rustic look, I see. Very… authentic." Suddenly, you're wondering if you've been insulted or if you're just overly sensitive.

Their motto? "Why say it directly when I can disguise it as a joke?"

How the Snide Sniper Operates

The Snide Sniper's tools of the trade are as sharp as their tongue. Here's how they keep everyone slightly on edge:

- **Backhanded Compliments:** "Oh, you made this yourself? I thought it came from the store. Impressive!"

- **Deflecting Criticism:** If anyone dares to call them out, they whip out the classic, "Relax, it's just a joke."

- **Targeted Strikes:** They have a knack for picking the perfect moment—and the perfect person—to deliver their snide remarks.

- **Stirring the Pot:** A well-placed quip can ignite a ripple of tension, and the Snide Sniper sits back to enjoy the fireworks.

Snide Sniper in Action

Let's set the scene: The family is gathered around, complimenting the turkey. It's all warm fuzzies until the Snide Sniper pipes up.

Snide Sniper: *"Wow, it's actually good this year! Did you use a different recipe—or just get lucky?"*

Cue the awkward pause as everyone silently debates whether to laugh, defend the turkey, or simply pretend the comment didn't happen.

How They Drain Your Energy

Blasting the Snide Sniper is like navigating a conversational minefield. Their quips might seem small, but they add up, leaving you bracing for their next remark instead of enjoying the moment. It's exhausting trying to dodge their verbal darts while keeping your spirits intact.

Tips for Spotting the Snide Sniper

You'll know the Snide Sniper when you hear their favorite phrases:

- "I'm just saying…"

- "Oh, don't take it so seriously."

- "It's just a joke—you're so sensitive."

They also have a trademark smirk, often paired with a quick glance to assess just how much their comment landed.

Blasting the Snide Sniper

The good news? You don't have to let the Snide Sniper's comments ruin your Thanksgiving vibe. Here's how to handle them without breaking a sweat:

- **Call Them Out Lightly:** A playful "Ouch, that one had teeth!" lets them know you noticed without escalating the situation.

- **Stay Confident:** Don't let their quips shake your self-assurance. A calm, "I'm really happy with how it turned out, thanks," is a perfect response.

- **Redirect the Conversation:** Shift the focus to something neutral and upbeat. "Anyway, who wants seconds?"

- **Don't Feed Their Fire:** Sarcasm thrives on reactions, so the less attention you give them, the less fuel they have.

The Takeaway

The Snide Sniper isn't here to ruin Thanksgiving—they're just addicted to being the sharpest tongue at the table. By keeping your cool, brushing off their remarks with humor, and steering conversations toward positivity, you can keep their snark from casting a shadow over your holiday.

So, when the Snide Sniper fires off a comment about your pie, your centerpiece, or your "unique" sense of style, remember: their words only have power if you let them. Thanksgiving is about gratitude and connection—not dodging verbal darts. Smile, pass the gravy, and let their quips roll off your back like butter on a hot biscuit.

The Inner Imp

"Are you sure you belong here? Everyone's judging you."

Of all the Energy Vampires at the Thanksgiving table, the Inner Imp is the sneakiest. It doesn't sit across from you or critique your turkey—it lives in your own head, whispering doubts and stirring up insecurities faster than Aunt Linda can stir the gravy. This tiny terror doesn't need to crash your party because it's already got a VIP seat in your mind, ready to sabotage your holiday cheer from the inside out.

Who Is the Inner Imp?

The Inner Imp is the ultimate Thanksgiving buzzkill. It specializes in making mountains out of mashed potato molehills and convincing you that everyone is secretly judging your cranberry sauce. While the other Energy Vampires bring external chaos, the Inner Imp works from within, making you doubt yourself at every turn.

Picture this: You're carving the turkey, and everything's going fine until the Inner Imp pipes up. "Are you sure you're doing that right?

Everyone's staring at you. They're probably laughing on the inside." Suddenly, you're sweating over a bird like it's a high-stakes cooking competition.

Its motto? "Why enjoy the holiday when you could spiral instead?"

How the Inner Imp Operates

The Inner Imp is a master of self-doubt and sabotage. Here's how it thrives:

- **Planting Doubts:** "Did you really just say that? They're totally judging you."

- **Amplifying Criticism:** "Aunt Linda said the pie was 'interesting.' She *hates* it. You should've bought one instead."

- **Highlighting Flaws:** "That stain on your shirt? Everyone noticed, and now they're talking about it."

- **Comparing to Others:** "Cousin Sarah has a perfect family, perfect job, and perfect pie. Why don't you?"

The Inner Imp in Action: A Case Study

Let's set the scene: You're enjoying a rare moment of calm, sipping some cider, when the Inner Imp decides it's time for a little chaos.

Inner Imp: *"Did you really just laugh that loudly at Uncle Joe's joke? Everyone thinks you're overdoing it. Tone it down, or they'll think you're weird."*

Cue the spiral of overthinking as you suddenly question every laugh, every gesture, and every glance around the room.

How It Drains Your Energy

The Inner Imp doesn't just drain your energy—it hijacks your entire mindset. Instead of soaking in the holiday joy, you're stuck battling an internal critic that doesn't know when to shut up. By the time dessert rolls around, you're too emotionally exhausted to even enjoy the pie.

Tips for Spotting the Inner Imp

The Inner Imp loves to disguise its whispers as helpful advice, but its favorite phrases give it away:

- "Are you sure that's enough?"

- "Everyone else has it together—why don't you?"

- "If you mess this up, it's going to be a disaster."

It also has impeccable timing, always popping up during quiet moments when you're most vulnerable.

Blasting the Inner Imp

The good news? You can silence the Inner Imp and take back control of your holiday cheer. Here's how to send it packing:

- **Name It and Shame It:** Recognize the Inner Imp for what it is—a pesky voice, not the truth. Call it out with, "Oh, it's *you* again. Thanks for stopping by, but I'm busy enjoying Thanksgiving."

- **Counter with Gratitude:** When the Inner Imp focuses on flaws, counter with gratitude. "Sure, the rolls are a little overbaked, but everyone's laughing and having a great time."

- **Practice Self-Compassion:** Treat yourself like you would a friend. "Hey, it's okay if the turkey isn't perfect. It's about the effort and the love, not the presentation."

- **Stay Present:** The Inner Imp loves to drag you into a spiral of overthinking. Focus on the here and now—what you see, hear, and smell—rather than the imaginary disasters it's cooking up.

The Takeaway

The Inner Imp isn't here to ruin your Thanksgiving on purpose—it's just really bad at staying quiet. By recognizing its tricks and refusing to let it take over, you can keep your holiday focused on joy, gratitude, and connection.

So, when the Inner Imp starts whispering about your laugh, your pie, or your ability to carve a turkey, remember: you're doing just fine. Thanksgiving isn't about perfection; it's about showing up, sharing love, and savoring the moment (and maybe an extra slice of pie). Tell the Inner Imp to take a hike and enjoy your holiday guilt-free—you've earned it!

The Inner Vampire

"Why even try? You know you're going to mess it up."

Lurking deep within each of us is the sneakiest Energy Vampire of all: the Inner Vampire. It's the shadowy voice in your head that magnifies your flaws, amplifies your fears, and makes you second-guess every decision. Unlike the other Energy Vampires at the table, the Inner Vampire doesn't need an invitation—it's already there, whispering doubts while you're basting the turkey or fretting over seating arrangements.

Who Is the Inner Vampire?

The Inner Vampire is your personal critic, anxiety factory, and guilt-tripper all rolled into one. It's not loud or flashy like the Drama Llama or as snarky as the Snide Sniper; it's subtle, weaving its way into your thoughts until you're convinced its criticisms are reality. Whether it's Thanksgiving or just a random Tuesday, the Inner Vampire loves to feast on your confidence, leaving you drained and doubting yourself.

Picture this: You're setting the table, and suddenly the Inner Vampire chimes in. "Are these plates too mismatched? Everyone's going to notice. They'll think you didn't even try." Suddenly, your carefully chosen table settings feel like a crime against dinnerware.

Its motto? "Why let you enjoy the moment when I can ruin it for you?"

How the Inner Vampire Operates

The Inner Vampire works quietly but efficiently, chipping away at your self-assurance one thought at a time. Here's how it thrives:

- **Perfectionist Poison:** "The gravy has a lump? Great, now the whole meal is ruined."

- **Comparison Chaos:** "Look at Sarah's Instagram—her table looks like it's straight out of a magazine. Yours looks like it came from a yard sale."

- **Fear Amplifier:** "What if the turkey's dry? What if they hate the pie? What if everyone secretly wishes they'd gone to Aunt Linda's instead?"

- **Guilt Grenade:** "Remember that Thanksgiving five years ago when you forgot the stuffing? Bet they all do too."

The Inner Vampire During Thanksgiving

Thanksgiving is like Disneyland for the Inner Vampire—so many opportunities to poke at your insecurities! Here's where it really shines:

- **While Cooking:** Every stir, every seasoning, every oven timer is met with whispers of, "Are you sure this is going to taste good? Everyone's expecting perfection, and this isn't it."

- **At the Table:** As everyone digs in, the Inner Vampire kicks into high gear. "Did you see the way Uncle Joe looked at the turkey? He probably thinks it's overcooked. You should've brined it longer."

- **During Conversations:** When you share a story, the Inner Vampire follows up with, "That was boring. Why would they care about that? Now they all think you're awkward."

- **After Everyone Leaves:** While you're cleaning up, it delivers the final blow: "You didn't do enough. No one really enjoyed it. Next year, they'll probably make other plans."

How the Inner Vampire Drains Your Energy

Blasting the Inner Vampire is like hosting a guest who criticizes your decor, eats all the snacks, and never leaves. It doesn't just zap your energy—it takes the joy out of every moment. Instead of focusing on laughter and connection, you're busy battling self-doubt and trying to fix imaginary problems.

Tips for Spotting the Inner Vampire

The Inner Vampire is tricky, but its favorite phrases give it away:

- "You're not good enough."
- "They're all judging you."
- "Why did you even bother trying?"
- "They'd all be happier somewhere else."

It loves to strike when you're already stressed, tired, or overwhelmed, making its whispers feel louder and more convincing.

Blasting the Inner Vampire

The good news? You don't have to let the Inner Vampire ruin your Thanksgiving—or your life. Here's how to show it the door:

- **Name It:** Recognize the Inner Vampire for what it is. Say, "Oh, hello again, Inner Vampire. Thanks for your input, but I'm not taking your advice today."
- **Challenge It:** When it whispers, "Everyone's judging you," counter with, "Or maybe they're just enjoying the meal and not overanalyzing everything like I am."
- **Practice Gratitude:** Gratitude is the Inner Vampire's kryptonite. Focus on what's going well: "The turkey might not be perfect, but everyone's laughing and having a good time—that's what matters."

- **Stay Present:** The Inner Vampire thrives on imaginary disasters and past mistakes. Ground yourself in the moment by noticing the sounds, smells, and joy around you.

The Takeaway

The Inner Vampire isn't here to help—it's here to hold you back. By recognizing its tricks and refusing to give it power, you can reclaim your confidence and enjoy Thanksgiving for what it's really about: love, gratitude, and connection.

So, when the Inner Vampire starts whispering about your gravy, your centerpiece, or your social skills, remind it who's in charge. Thanksgiving doesn't have to be perfect to be wonderful, and neither do you. Embrace the imperfections, laugh off the lumps in the gravy, and savor every bite, because you're doing just fine—Inner Vampire be damned!

Own Your Pie and Eat It Too

Thanksgiving is all about gratitude, and gratitude's secret sidekick—personal responsibility. After all, the Inner Vampire loves to whisper doubts and excuses, but personal responsibility is the voice that says, "Hold on—I've got this." It's about owning your choices, your reactions, and even your mistakes with a spirit of gratitude for the one thing you can always control: yourself. And once you embrace it, you'll see that personal responsibility isn't a burden—it's the key to savoring the best moments, pie included.

Why? Because owning your actions, reactions, and choices gives you the power to shape your experience. And, honestly, wouldn't you rather be the person steering the gravy boat of your life than the one watching it spill all over the table?

Here's the playful truth: taking responsibility isn't about blaming yourself when things go sideways (looking at you, slightly burnt stuffing). It's about recognizing that you control how you respond to those sideways moments. When the Drama Llama is in full meltdown mode or the Snide Sniper lands a zinger about your mashed potatoes, personal responsibility says, "Hey, you can't control their antics, but you *can* control how much of your energy you let them take."

Personal Responsibility at Thanksgiving

Let's say Aunt Linda's cranberry sauce critiques are hitting a little too close to home. You could stew over her comments all dinner long (wasting valuable pie-eating energy), or you could take responsibility for how you respond. Maybe you laugh it off with a quick, "Thanks for the feedback, Linda. I'll be sure to consult the cranberry council next year." Or just nod and savor your perfectly fine cranberry sauce.

The point is, personal responsibility isn't about being perfect—it's about keeping your cool, your joy, and your pie when Energy Vampires come knocking.

Why It's Fun (Yes, Really)

Here's where personal responsibility gets surprisingly fun: it puts you in the driver's seat. Instead of being at the mercy of everyone else's drama or negativity, you get to decide how the story plays out. It's like having a backstage pass to your own life, where you call the shots on what gets your attention and what doesn't.

And when you realize you have that power, the Energy Vampires suddenly lose their bite. The Drama Llama? Hilarious. The Snide Sniper? Meh, whatever. The Inner Vampire? Bring it on, you've got this.

The Takeaway

Personal responsibility isn't a chore—it's a superpower. It's what lets you enjoy Thanksgiving (and life) without getting sucked into the chaos swirling around you. So, this year, own your choices, embrace your quirks, and laugh off the imperfections. Because when you take responsibility for your energy, your attitude, and your joy, no Energy Vampire can touch you.

And let's face it—nothing's more satisfying than that second helping of pumpkin pie *you chose* to enjoy guilt-free.

Just Giggle

There's something downright liberating about surviving Thanksgiving's emotional buffet—complete with side dishes of family drama, a helping of burnt stuffing, and the inevitable turkey mishap—and just… giggling. Yes, giggling! Not the polite kind that you use to humor Aunt Carol, but the real, soul-shaking kind that bubbles up from your core, like gravy bubbling on the stove. It's the sound of triumph, of joy, and, let's face it, relief.

Giggle Yoga isn't about yoga mats or poses—it's about stretching your humor muscles and finding the funny in all the turkey-fueled chaos. It's the practice of laughing at life's absurdities, especially when they happen at the Thanksgiving table. Because let's be honest: life is one giant comedy, and Thanksgiving is the annual highlight reel.

Think about it. Uncle Bob's annual rant about "the good old days." The Judgy Judy Vampire sneaking in a passive-aggressive "Oh, you're *still* single?" The turkey that looks less golden brown and more, well, crispy black. And yet, in the middle of it all, there's laughter just waiting to burst out. That's the essence of Giggle Yoga—taking the chaos, the drama, and even the gravy stains, and turning them into reasons to laugh.

The Art of the Thanksgiving Giggle

Giggle Yoga is a mindset, a holiday survival skill, and quite possibly your best weapon against the Energy Vampires lurking around the table. The Inner Vampire might whisper, "You didn't make enough pie," but a good giggle silences it faster than you can say "pass the whipped cream." The Drama Lama Vampire may try to stir up an argument over politics, but Giggle Yoga turns that tension into comedy gold.

Here's how it works: Instead of groaning at life's mishaps, you giggle. When the turkey comes out looking "artisanal" (aka unevenly cooked), giggle. When Aunt Carol unveils her mystery casserole (again), giggle. When the mashed potatoes hit the floor, giggle and call it abstract art. Giggle Yoga is about finding humor in the things you can't control and laughing at the things you can.

Giggling Through Gratitude

Thanksgiving is all about gratitude, and Giggle Yoga is gratitude's secret sidekick. Gratitude says, "Wow, I'm so thankful for this pie," and Giggle Yoga adds, "Even if it looks like it's been through a pie fight." Together, they're an unstoppable duo. Gratitude keeps you grounded, and giggling keeps you light.

When you giggle, you remind yourself that the little hiccups—like the cranberry sauce nobody eats or the gravy boat that spills—are part of what makes life, and Thanksgiving, perfectly imperfect. It's about laughing through the messiness and embracing the beauty of the moment.

Why Giggling Works

Let's be real: it's impossible to hold onto stress, resentment, or tension when you're genuinely giggling. A good giggle releases more tension than a post-Thanksgiving nap. It brings you back to the present moment, reminding you that life isn't just a collection of to-do lists and expectations. It's also a comedy show, and you're the star.

So, as you sit down to your Thanksgiving feast, ready to face the Energy Vampires and the quirks of your family, remember this: giggling isn't just a reaction—it's a choice. A choice to embrace the chaos, laugh at the imperfections, and enjoy the journey.

This Thanksgiving, make Giggle Yoga your holiday tradition. Laugh at the turkey that looks a little "extra crispy." Giggle at the gravy boat's dramatic spill. And most importantly, giggle with the people around the table—because laughter is the glue that holds us all together, even when the mashed potatoes fall apart.

Let your giggles be loud, contagious, and unapologetic. Because when you giggle, you're not just surviving Thanksgiving—you're celebrating it. And isn't that what this holiday is all about? Pass the pie, and pass the laughter, because this Thanksgiving, you're giggling your way to joy.

10 Steps to Giggle Like a Pro

Ready to master Giggle Yoga and take down those Energy Vampires with a laugh? Here are ten easy steps to flex those humor muscles and find your giggle groove, no matter how chaotic the turkey table gets.

The Snort Starter

Think of something mildly funny, then exaggerate it in your mind. Uncle Bob's comb-over? Imagine it blowing in the wind like a superhero cape. Boom—instant giggle spark. Bonus points if you snort while laughing; it's contagious.

The Belly Shaker

Channel your inner Santa Claus and give yourself permission to laugh from the gut. The louder and jollier, the better. Even if the joke's on you, own it—because a belly laugh is like a full-body stretch for your spirit.

The Silent Screamer

For those moments when laughing out loud isn't socially acceptable (looking at you, dinner prayer), go full silent mode. Shake your shoulders, gasp for air, and make your eyes wide—it's hilarious, and nobody will know why you're crying into your mashed potatoes.

The Giggle Relay

Pass the giggle baton. Start with a small chuckle and make eye contact with someone who needs a laugh. Watch as your laughter spreads across the table like gravy on a plate. This is especially effective with kids and slightly tipsy relatives.

The Cringe Flip

Turn awkward moments into giggle gold. Did someone just bring up politics? Pretend they're auditioning for a reality show called *Thanksgiving: The Drama Lama Edition*. Picture the title card in your head. Now laugh.

The Fake-It-Till-You-Giggle

Even if you don't feel like laughing, fake it. Start with a "ha-ha" that sounds like a bad acting audition, and before you know it, you'll be rolling. Laughter doesn't care if it's real or fake—it works either way.

The Giggling Gratitude Bomb

When the Energy Vampires start to creep in, drop a giggling gratitude bomb. Say something absurdly thankful, like, "I'm so grateful we have forks to eat this pie instead of our hands." It'll catch people off guard and turn tension into giggles.

The Dad Joke Gambit

Keep a dad joke locked and loaded for emergencies. Example: "What did the turkey say to the vampire? Stop gobbling up all my energy!" It's so bad, it's good. Watch the eye-rolls turn into grins.

The Power Pose Giggle

Stand tall, throw your arms wide, and let out a triumphant laugh, even if it's just in your head. This is the ultimate mood booster—it tells your brain you're winning, no matter what's burning in the oven.

The Pie Punchline

Save your best laugh for dessert. By then, everyone's full, relaxed, and ready for a good laugh. Whether it's a pumpkin pie mishap or someone sneakily eating the last piece, lean into the humor of it. Remember, laughter is the sweetest dish on the table.

So, there you have it—ten ways to giggle your way through Thanksgiving. With these moves, you'll not only blast Energy Vampires into glittery oblivion, but you'll also be the hero of the holiday. Laughter really is the best vampire repellent—and it pairs perfectly with pie.

Wrapping Up the Feast - Vampires Vanquished!

Congratulations, brave soul—you've made it through Thanksgiving with a table full of food *and* Energy Vampires. From the Drama Llama spilling tea (and maybe gravy) to the Snide Sniper launching passive-aggressive zingers, you've faced them all. And let's not forget the Inner Vampire, always lurking, always whispering, "Are you *really* sure you're doing this right?" Spoiler alert: you were.

So, what have we learned?

The Energy Vampires Are Inevitable

The truth is, Energy Vampires are as much a part of Thanksgiving as pumpkin pie and unspoken family tension. Whether they're one-upping your stories, disappearing mid-conversation, or turning the dinner table into a soap opera set, they'll always find their way in. The key isn't to banish them (though the thought is tempting)—it's to outsmart them with grace, humor, and a pinch of garlic-level confidence.

The Inner Vampire Is the Craftiest of Them All

Sure, Aunt Linda's passive-aggressive cranberry comments sting, but the Inner Vampire? That one knows *all* your weak spots. It's the sneaky one, convincing you to doubt yourself even before the turkey hits the table. But guess what? You called it out. You saw through its tricks, and you didn't let it take the wheel. Take a bow—you've earned it.

Laughter Is the Best Garlic

You might not be able to stop the Drama Llama from spinning every spilled drink into a Shakespearean tragedy, but you *can* diffuse it with a little humor. A well-timed joke or a lighthearted deflection can disarm even the peskiest Energy Vampire. Plus, it's way more fun than rolling your eyes into oblivion.

Gratitude Is the Ultimate Vampire Blaster

At the end of the day (and the feast), the true magic of Thanksgiving isn't in perfect gravy or a flawless centerpiece—it's in the gratitude. Sure, the Energy Vampires tested your patience, but they also reminded you of something important: you can find joy, connection, and hilarity even in the chaos.

You're a Thanksgiving MVP

You handled the Drama Llama, redirected the Bicker Birds, outplayed the Snide Sniper, and silenced the Inner Vampire. You kept your energy intact (mostly) and managed to enjoy the day without flipping the table—though let's admit, the thought crossed your mind.

A Toast to You, the Energy Vampire Blaster Extraordinaire

As the dishes are cleared, the leftovers are packed, and the final crumbs of pie are devoured, take a moment to reflect on your victory. You didn't just survive Thanksgiving—you owned it.

- You stood tall against passive-aggressive pie critiques.

- You deflected meddling questions about your love life, career, or why you still don't have a dog.

- You handled your Inner Vampire like a pro, serving it a heaping plate of *not today, pal.*

So, here's to you: the energy master, the vampire slayer, the turkey champion. You've earned that second helping of stuffing and an uninterrupted nap on the couch.

And remember, the lessons learned today aren't just for Thanksgiving—they're for every holiday, family gathering, or random Tuesday when Energy Vampires creep into your life. Because now, you know their tricks, and you've got the tools to keep your joy intact.

Now, go enjoy that leftover pumpkin pie—guilt-free, vampire-free, and absolutely fabulous. Cheers!

Quick Comebacks for Thanksgiving Energy Vampires

"Serving Sass with a Smile"

The Drama Llama

- *"Hold on, let me grab some popcorn for this Oscar-worthy meltdown."*

- *"Wow, that's intense! Are we still talking about spilled gravy?"*

The Pessimist Pilgrim

- *"Good to know your glass isn't just half-empty—it's cracked, too."*

- *"Can we get you a gratitude list, or is that too optimistic?"*

The Nosy Nester

- *"Oh, you're writing a biography about me? You should've said so!"*
- *"I'd love to answer that, but my lawyer said I shouldn't."*

The Bragging Butterball

- *"Wow, it must be exhausting being so amazing all the time!"*
- *"I'm impressed you found a way to make my story about you—talent!"*

The One-Up Turkey

- *"Oh, you win. I'll be sure to send you the trophy in the mail."*
- *"I didn't realize this was a competition! Hold on while I lower my expectations."*

The Gloom Monger

- *"You're right—it's all downhill from here. Want to slide together?"*
- *"I hear they're giving free hugs at the optimist's table. Shall we go?"*

The Sullen Teen

- *"Careful, if you smile, your face might get stuck like that!"*
- *"Don't worry, we'll wait until you're ready to grace us with your presence."*

The Bicker Birds

- *"Hold on, let me grab a referee shirt before this gets serious."*
- *"This is riveting—can we make it a podcast so I can replay it later?"*

The Judgy Judy

- *"Oh, I didn't realize you were Yelp for Thanksgiving. What's my rating?"*
- *"Thanks for the feedback! I'll be sure to file that under 'Who Asked You?'"*

The Ghosting

- *"Oh, you're back! We were about to put your face on a milk carton."*

- *"Don't worry, we'll recap everything you missed in a detailed email."*

The Martyr Mom

- *"Wow, you've done so much! Should we start a slow clap now or wait?"*

- *"Don't worry—I hear they're giving out medals for 'Most Overworked.'"*

The Snide Sniper

- *"Ouch, that zinger had teeth! Did you sharpen it just for me?"*

- *"Your wit is like gravy—thick and unnecessary."*

The Inner Imp

- *"Thanks for your input, Inner Imp, but I'll take it from here."*

- *"Oh, it's you again. I'll listen to you right after I finish ignoring you."*

Thanksgiving Jokes to Gobble Up

Why don't Energy Vampires ever bring food to Thanksgiving?

Because they're already full of drama and complaints.

What's an Energy Vampire's favorite Thanksgiving side dish?

Mashed doubts and gravy guilt.

Why did the Inner Vampire refuse the turkey?

It was too dry, just like its sense of optimism.

How do you know an Energy Vampire is at your Thanksgiving table?

They're the ones turning the cranberry sauce into a heated debate.

What do you call it when the Bicker Birds fight over the last roll?

A breadwinner battle.

Why did the Snide Sniper bring their own gravy?

So they could pour their sarcasm on everything else.

How do you serve stuffing to an Energy Vampire?

With a side of boundaries and a dollop of humor.

Why did the Drama Llama skip dessert?

It had enough pie—*of everyone's attention.*

How does the Pessimist Pilgrim describe Thanksgiving?

"Turkey's good, but we'll probably all run out of food by next year."

Why doesn't the Martyr Mom play Thanksgiving games?

She's too busy winning gold in the "I do everything" Olympics.

What's the Ghosting's favorite Thanksgiving tradition?

Leaving before the dishes are even cleared.

Why did the Nosy Nester sit closest to the turkey?

To find out all the juicy details of its roasting process.

What did the Inner Imp say to the pumpkin pie?

"Not bad, but I bet Sarah's pie is better."

What's an Energy Vampire's favorite thing to bring to dinner?

Complaints—it pairs well with every course.

Why don't Energy Vampires like gravy?

Because it smooths things over, and they *live* for the lumps.

What do you call an Energy Vampire that eats too much turkey?

The Nap Master—they're out before the drama starts.

How does the Bragging Butterball describe their Thanksgiving?

"The best turkey, the best sides, the best family—*obviously*."

What did the Judgy Judy say about the table settings?

"Paper napkins? Bold move. I guess some people are into rustic."

Why did the One-Up Turkey carve their own bird?

"Because last year, I carved three turkeys in under an hour."

How do you keep an Energy Vampire out of your mashed potatoes?

Tell them it's seasoned with positivity—they'll stay far away!

"Am I the Energy Vampire? I mean, I did bring up politics over the mashed potatoes… so, yeah, probably."

"I told myself I wouldn't eat too much and complain about it later, but here I am—stuffed and whining like a true Thanksgiving cliché."

"I think I'm the Snide Sniper this year. My cranberry sauce critique really hit Aunt Linda in the feels. Oops."

"I might be the Drama Llama. I spilled gravy and turned it into a three-act tragedy."

"Turns out I'm the Ghosting. I vanished the second dishes needed washing and reappeared just in time for pie. Classic me."

"My Inner Vampire told me not to share that story at dinner. Now I'm replaying it in my head on a loop like a cringe highlight reel."

"My Inner Vampire whispered, 'Don't try to carve the turkey; you'll mess it up.' So naturally, I grabbed the knife and proved it right."

"My Inner Vampire showed up before dinner and said, 'Don't over-think it.' Joke's on them—I'm still overthinking it *and* the dessert options."

"The Inner Vampire strikes again: I tried to toast the family, but instead, I thanked the turkey for its service."

"I asked my Inner Vampire if the pie looked okay, and it said, 'Sure, if you like pie with personality flaws.'"

Game: "Pass the Pumpkin of Positivity"

Objective

B ring laughter, connection, and a little lighthearted chaos to the Thanksgiving table by turning a pumpkin (or any small object) into the centerpiece of a quick-thinking, feel-good game.

What You'll Need

A mini pumpkin (real or decorative), a roll, or anything small and throwable (preferably soft—no injuries, please). A timer (or someone with good judgment to yell "time's up!").

How to Play

Set the Scene: Begin by explaining that the goal of the game is to keep the pumpkin moving around the table while completing a fun prompt. Each person gets only *five seconds* to answer before they pass the pumpkin to the next player.

The Prompts: Players answer prompts that change each round. Start with lighthearted prompts and gradually get sillier or more heartfelt:

- "Say one thing you're grateful for."
- "Give a funny nickname to the person on your left."
- "What's one 'Energy Vampire' habit you're guilty of?"
- "Make a Thanksgiving-themed animal sound."
- "Invent a weird Thanksgiving dish you'd *never* eat."

The Rules: The pumpkin starts with one player who answers the prompt and then tosses (gently!) the pumpkin to someone else. If you hesitate for more than *five seconds* or repeat someone else's answer, you're "stuffed"! "Stuffed" players must perform a fun forfeit, like gobbling like a turkey, making a dramatic apology to the pumpkin, or explaining why their mashed potatoes are secretly judging them.

Winner Takes the Pie

The game ends when everyone has completed at least one round without being "stuffed," or when the dessert is served. The winner is the person who never gets "stuffed" or makes the best save during their forfeit.

Why It's Fun

This game keeps things playful, encourages creativity, and turns the spotlight onto everyone equally. It's also a sneaky way to diffuse tension and keep those Energy Vampires at bay with humor and connection.

Now, grab the pumpkin and let the chaos (and laughs) begin! Let me know if you'd like any further tweaks!

David's Other Books

Footsteps After the Fall

Dancing with Energy Vampires

Second Mouse Gets the Cheese

What if Today Were the Day?

Who are you fooling?

Egg Nog. Elves. Oy Vey.

Valentines Energy Vampire Detox

Halloween Energy Vampire Blasters

Going Bananas with Dementia

David's 1st Book

David's 2nd Book

David's 3rd Book

SECOND MOUSE
GETS THE CHEESE

FEELING TRAPPED BY MISTAKES, BAD ADVICE OR INEXPERIENCE?

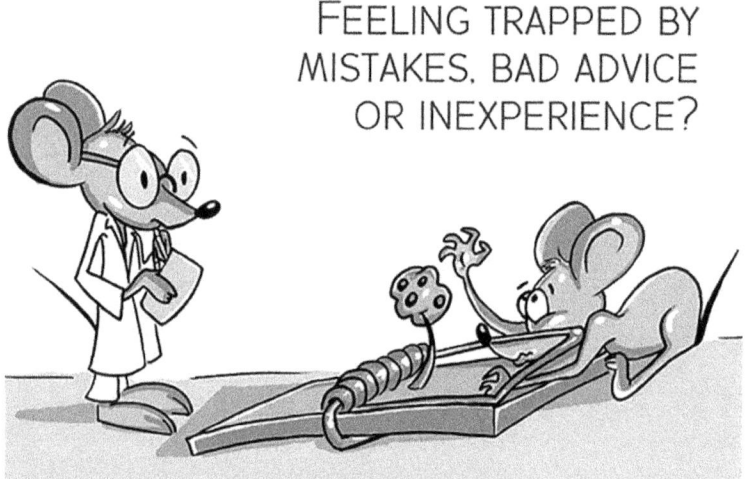

Upgrade your thinking
Make smarter decisions
Build strong relationships

DAVID LLOYD STRAUSS

David's 4th Book

WHAT *if* TODAY *were the* DAY?

a pocket book by
DAVID LLOYD STRAUSS

David's 5th Book

David's 6th Book

Egg Nog, Elves & Oy Vey!

Holiday Family Drama Survival Guide

DAVID LLOYD STRAUSS

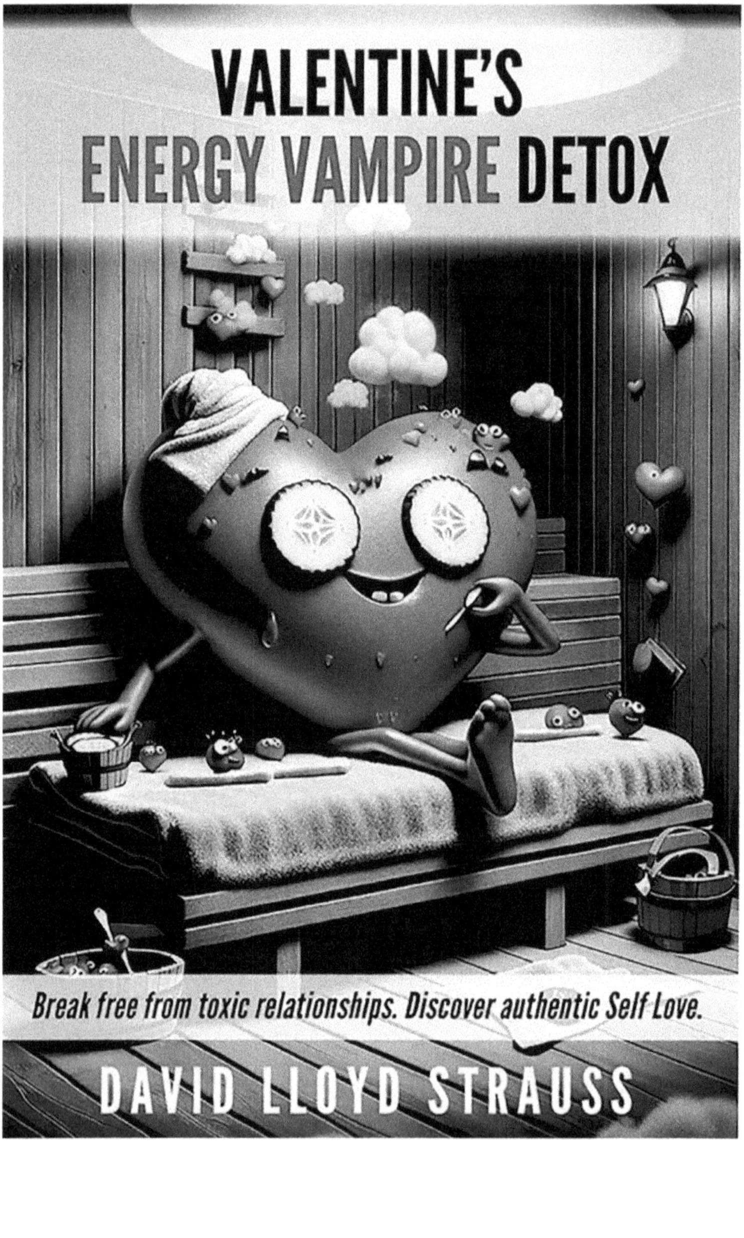

David's 8th Book

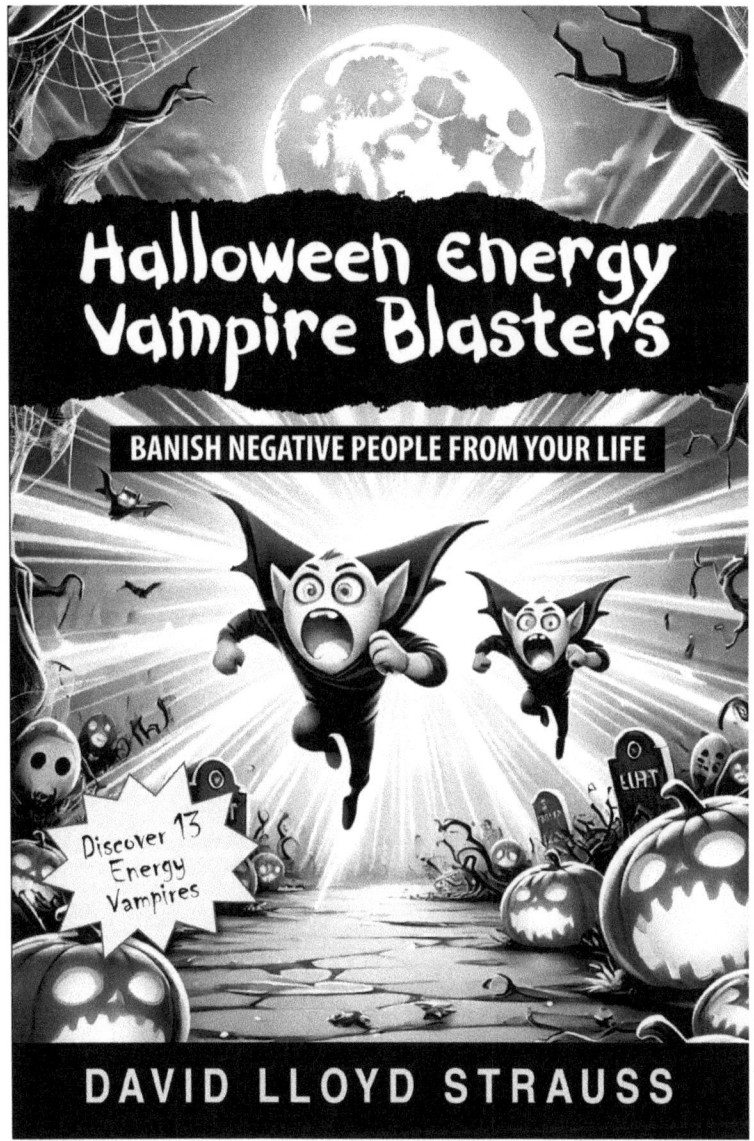

David's 9th Book

Write That Book Already

Let David Strauss help you write and publish your book!

Author Coaching · Ghosting Writing

Editing · Publishing

Done for you OR Done with you!

Go to: DavidStrauss.com

About the Author

"Finding Purpose After a Falling Rock and Brush with Death."

When a falling rock struck David Strauss on the head at the ancient ruins of Chaco Canyon, New Mexico, it wasn't just an accident—it was a life-altering wake-up call. What started as a near-death experience became a second chance to rediscover what truly matters. His harrowing walk through the desert with an open head injury and concussion turned into a powerful metaphor for resilience and determination—the very qualities that now define his life and work.

During his years of recovery, David embraced this second chance, uncovering a purpose bigger than himself. Fueled by a commitment to helping others, he began sharing the lessons he learned about self-responsibility, inner strength, and how to find joy, even when life feels impossibly hard.

David has written more than nine books, each offering practical insights and heartfelt wisdom from his own journey. Titles like Footsteps After the Fall and What If Today Were the Day bring lightheartedness to self-discovery, while Energy Vampire Blasters teaches readers how to protect their energy and curate relationships that uplift rather than drain. His work proves that transformation is possible—even when life throws you its toughest curveballs.

David has also discovered a niche that gives his life deeper purpose: helping others write and publish their personal stories of growth and transformation. Guiding people to turn their struggles into stories of inspiration isn't just his passion—it's his way of paying forward the second chance he was given.

David lives by the Giggle Yoga Philosophy, which emphasizes mental, emotional, and spiritual flexibility, personal responsibility, and the joy of contributing to something greater than oneself. This philosophy infuses his work with a unique blend of humor, wisdom, and heart, reminding others that a little laughter can make even life's hardest moments more bearable.

Today, David uses his story to inspire others to tap into their own resilience and live with intention. Whether he's speaking at events like the Global Entrepreneurship Initiative at the United Nations Headquarters, collaborating with individuals to share their journeys, or connecting with readers through his books, his down-to-earth approach and genuine love for people shine in everything he does.

David isn't just telling his story—he's living proof that a near-death experience can become a spark for joy, connection, and personal growth. Through his writing, speaking, and mentoring, David empowers others to see life not as something that happens to them, but as something they can create, one purposeful choice at a time.

DavidStrauss.com

INSTAGRAM: IAMDavidStrauss

LinkedIn: IAMDavidStrauss